drape drape 3

Hisako Sato

Laurence King Publishing

LAURENCE KING

Published in 2013 by
Laurence King Publishing Ltd
361–373 City Road
London EC1V 1LR
United Kingdom
Tel: + 44 20 7841 6900
Fax: + 44 20 7841 6910
e-mail: enquiries@laurenceking.com
www.laurenceking.com

Drape Drape 3 by Hisako Sato
Copyright © Hisako Sato 2011
Original Japanese edition published by EDUCATIONAL FOUNDATION BUNKA
GAKUEN, BUNKA PUBLISHING BUREAU.

This English edition is published by arrangement with EDUCATIONAL FOUNDATION
BUNKA GAKUEN, BUNKA PUBLISHING BUREAU, Tokyo, in care of Tuttle-Mori
Agency, Inc., Tokyo.

Hisako Sato has asserted her right under the Copyright, Designs, and Patent Act 1988,
to be identified as the Author of this Work.

A catalogue record for this book is available from the British Library.

ISBN: 978-1-78067-100-0

Typeface: Sabon and Syntax
Printed in China

Hisako Sato

Hisako Sato graduated from the Fashion Design program at Bunka
Fashion College, Japan, in 1986, leaving to work for a major apparel
manufacturer. In 1990, she was appointed head of garment design at
Muji, before becoming an independent designer in 1993. In 1994,
Hisako Sato made her debut at Tokyo Collection (now Japan Fashion
Week) with the Beige shop brand. She is currently producing new
collections as a designer for the Raw+ brand: www.rawtus.com

Contents

There are limitless variations to the designs you can produce through draping. It is an endlessly versatile technique, in which beautiful, cascading forms find expression in the draped design elements that come together to create the garment as a whole.

Drape Drape 3 introduces a new set of techniques to your designs, including twisted, crossed, and knotted effects.

I hope you'll have fun working with different patterns and fabrics to create these designs, which feature a range of draped effects from the very simple to the lavish and extravagant.

Once you get to work, I think you'll be pleasantly surprised by how easy and enjoyable draped designs can be to make.

no. 7 two-piece v-neck blouse
+ no. 8 three-piece tuck drape shorts
see pages 42, 44 for instructions

How to make the garments

About sizes and the full-scale patterns included with this book

You will find full-scale patterns for all of the garments presented in *Drape Drape 3* at the back of this book. While some of the designs are for one-size garments, others can be made in either two sizes (S/M and L/XL), or four sizes (S, M, L, and XL). Please consult the size chart when choosing the pattern size.

The full-scale patterns all include seam allowances. Be careful when copying the patterns; the shape of the seam allowances and position of the notches are very important when folding tucks and creating other effects.

In *Drape Drape 3* I have revisited the techniques featured in the earlier volumes in this series, *Drape Drape* and *Drape Drape 2*. This time, though, I have taken ideas such as slack (photograph 1), tucks (photograph 2), gathers (photograph 3), and combinations of these techniques (photograph 4), and given them a twist effect (photographs 5 and 6) or added a knottable string feature (photograph 7).

The designs use a variety of fabrics—cottons, wools, tricots (jerseys), and silks—in print, lace, and other forms. The best way to achieve garments identical to those shown in *Drape Drape 3* is to use the fabrics stated, though in many instances you may not be able to get hold of the exact same ones. The flow and volume of the drape will change somewhat with the fabric used, which can only add to the fun of making the garments!

Size chart (cm)					
	Size	S	M	L	XL
	Height	153	158	163	168
Body	Bust	78	82	86	90
measurements	Waist	58	62	66	70
	Hips	84	88	92	96

1

2

3

4

5

6
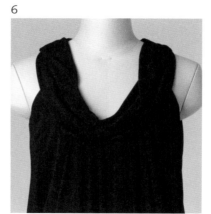

7

Fabrics

Woven fabrics made from cotton and wool are not difficult to handle. However, knitted fabrics such as doubleknit (double rib) (photograph 1) and jersey (plain knit) (photograph 2) that stretch even when made from cotton, wool, or silk, as well as tricots and other fabrics where the yarn itself is stretchy, demand different needles, thread, and methods of sewing. Make sure you have a needle and thread that are designed specifically for working with stretch fabrics, as this will allow you to sew most stretch fabrics more easily. I have covered ways to deal with stretch fabrics as well as woven fabrics below.

Preparation

1 Grain mending

Cotton and wool may shrink when exposed to steam or moisture from a steam iron, and the fabric itself may warp, so it makes sense to mend the grain before cutting.

With woven fabrics (photograph 3), first unravel the weft and cut straight along the raw edge. With lace fabrics that have no weft to remove (photograph 4), cut using the pattern of the fabric as a guide. In the case of knitted fabrics such as doubleknit (double rib) (photograph 1) and jersey (plain knit) (photograph 2), however, do not unravel the thread, whether the fabric is made from cotton, wool, or silk. Gently cut straight along the cross stitch instead.

Cotton should then be soaked for two to three hours and dried in a shaded place, without being wrung out. Iron while damp. If the raw edges do not meet when the fabric is folded in two to bring the selvages together, it means that the fabric has warped. Pull the fabric in the direction of the bias (diagonally to the warp) to adjust the grain, then iron. With wool, run a steam iron over the entire fabric, adjusting the grain so that the horizontal and vertical stitches become perpendicular. With silk, simply run a dry iron over the entire fabric to adjust the grain.

Doubleknit (double rib)—In lock-knits, the same stitch is visible on both right side (upside) and wrong side (reverse), and the raw edges lie flat.

Jersey (plain knit)—In flat-knits, the appearance of the stitch is different on the right side (upside) and wrong side (reverse). Raw edges are easily rolled to the right side (upside).

Sewing needles designed for use on stretch fabrics—Use a ball-point needle that is long from eye to tip. It will exert only a light pressure on the fabric, making it easy to sew and preventing the foundation yarn from breaking.

Thread to use with knitted fabrics—Use a nylon thread that will stretch ever so slightly to fit with the movements of the fabric, such as Gütermann, Resilon or Leona 66.

1

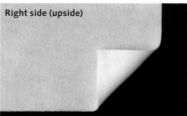

Right side (upside)

2

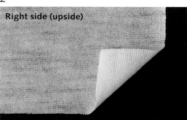

Right side (upside)

3

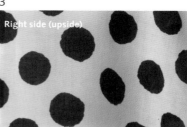

Right side (upside)

4

Right side (upside)

2 Cutting and marking

On symmetrical designs, fold the fabric in two on the outside, place the pattern (including the seam allowances) over it, and weigh it down. Add notches (of around 5 mm) to the markings, and indicate the cutting line with chalk (photograph 1). Gently remove the pattern without moving the two layers of fabric, and resecure the edge of the cutting line with marking pins. Cut with scissors following the marked cutting line. If the cloth slips noticeably as a result of being forced by the blades when using scissors to cut stretch fabrics, tricot (jersey), and other such fabrics in two layers, make a mark to the left and right of the cutting line on each layer to give improved cutting accuracy. Tack with tacking thread if you have a number of tucks that are difficult to make out using just notches. During this process, you can change the color of the tacking thread on the mountain and valley folds to ensure that the tuck is folded in the correct direction (see pattern for garment no. 1, figures A and B).

3 Interfacing

Attach fusible interfacing to the facing and other areas that you want to secure firmly. First align the fusible side with the wrong side (reverse) of the fabric and press lightly with a dry iron to secure temporarily in place. To ensure that the adhesive does not seep onto the iron from the fabric backing of the interfacing, cover with kraft or tracing paper or a damp cloth and iron firmly. Fabric with fusible interfacing can easily kink while cooling off, so take care not to move it. When applying woven fusible stay tape, place 2 to 3 mm over the stitching line on straight seam lines, such as shoulder lines, in order to prevent stretching. If you are applying tape to curved areas, such as armholes, first gently apply it to the outer circumference, where the measurement is longer, and then iron the fusible stay tape flat (photograph 3). In the case of stretch fabrics, apply knitted fusible stretch tape (photograph 4) if you want to fit the tape to the stretchiness of the fabric without actually stretching it. The area with the fusible stay tape will be surprisingly hard. I have not asked you to apply fusible stay tape to the neckline and armhole areas that will be hemmed, but if they do end up stretching, cut the tape finely so that it fits inside the width of the hemming when you apply it.

1

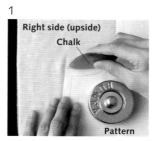

Right side (upside)
Chalk
Pattern

no. 1

Center back

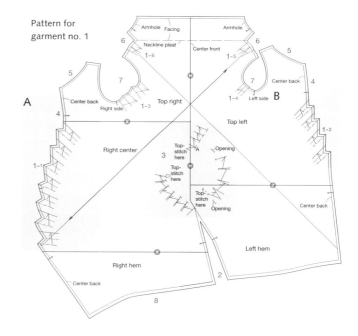

Pattern for garment no. 1

Armhole　Facing　Armhole
6　Neckline pleat　Center front　6　5
1-6　　1-5
5　7　Center back　4
7　Left side
A　Center back　1-4　B
4　Right side　1-3　Top right　Top left
　　　1-2
1-1　Right center　Top-stitch here　A　Opening
3　Top-stitch here
Top-stitch here　Center back
Opening
Left hem
Right hem　2
Center back
8

2

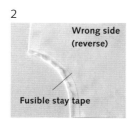

Wrong side (reverse)

Fusible stay tape

3

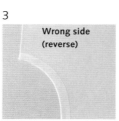

Wrong side (reverse)

4

A

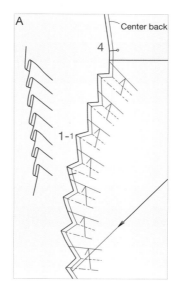

Center back
4
1-1

B

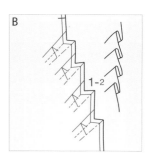

1-2

–·–·–·– Mountain fold
-------- Valley fold

no. 1 one-piece twist drape dress
see page 12 for instructions

no. 1 one-piece twist drape dress

◆ **Required pattern pieces (side A)**

1 Bodice (align the top right, center right, right hem, top left, and left hem)
* Trace the tuck positions

◆ **Sewing instructions**

* Attach fusible stay tape to the back neckline, the seam allowances on the armholes, and the wrong side (reverse) of the opening.
1 Fold the tucks in the center back, shoulders, and armholes (see figure 1 on p. 14).
2 Sew the dart in the front hem (see figure 2 on p. 14).
3 Fold the tucks at the center of the bodice to arrange the fabric into a twisted panel (see figure 3 on p. 15).
4 Sew the center back.
5 Finish the back neckline.
6 Finish the edge of the facing on the front neckline and sew the shoulders (see figure 6 on p. 15).
7 Finish the armholes.
8 Fold up the seam allowance on the hem and stitch.

◆ **Widths and lengths used**

Fabric: stretch fabric/jersey (plain knit)
= W 1 m 60 cm x L 1 m 60 cm
Fusible stay tape
= W 7 mm, length to suit

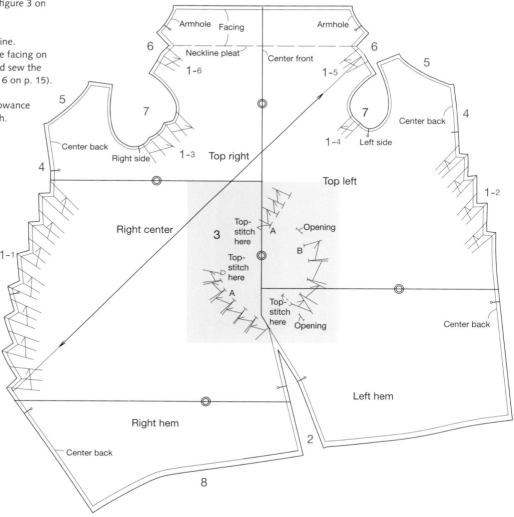

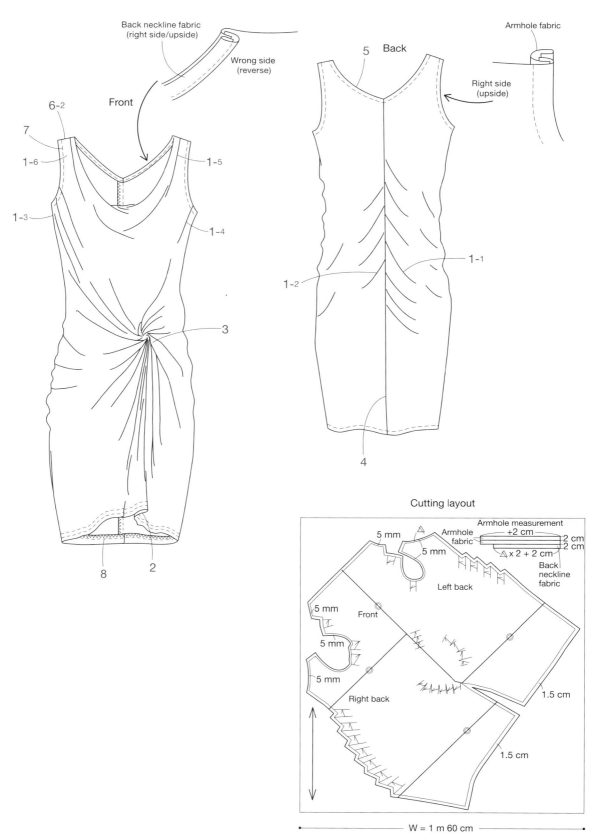

Back neckline fabric
(right side/upside)

Wrong side
(reverse)

Front

6-2

7

1-6

1-5

1-3

1-4

3

8   2

5   Back

Armhole fabric

Right side
(upside)

1-1

1-2

4

Cutting layout

5 mm

Armhole
fabric

5 mm

Armhole measurement
+2 cm

△ x 2 + 2 cm

2 cm
2 cm

Back
neckline
fabric

Left back

5 mm   Front

5 mm

5 mm

Right back

1.5 cm

1.5 cm

— W = 1 m 60 cm —

* Seam allowance is 1 cm, unless specified

13

1 Fold the tucks in the center back, shoulders, and armholes

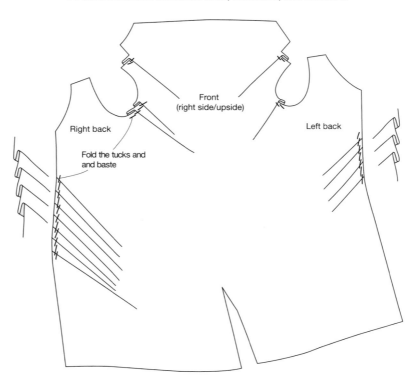

2 Sew the dart in the front hem

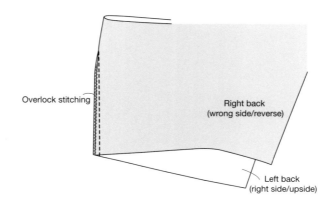

3 Fold the tucks at the center of the bodice to arrange the fabric into a twisted panel

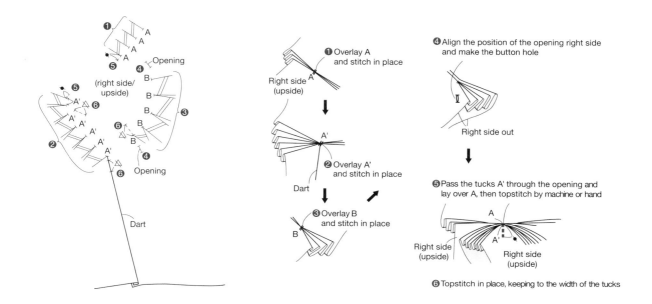

❶ Overlay A and stitch in place

Right side (upside)

❷ Overlay A' and stitch in place

Dart

❸ Overlay B and stitch in place

❹ Align the position of the opening right side and make the button hole

Right side out

❺ Pass the tucks A' through the opening and lay over A, then topstitch by machine or hand

A

Right side (upside)

A'

Right side (upside)

❻ Topstitch in place, keeping to the width of the tucks

6 Finish the edge of the facing on the front neckline and sew the shoulders

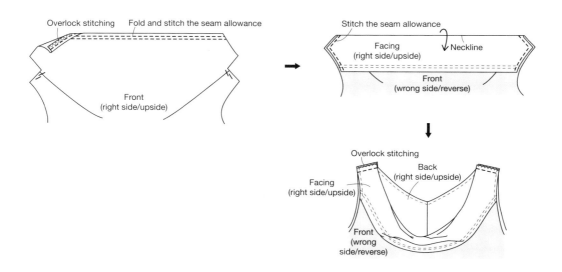

Overlock stitching   Fold and stitch the seam allowance

Front (right side/upside)

Stitch the seam allowance

Facing (right side/upside)

Neckline

Front (wrong side/reverse)

Overlock stitching

Back (right side/upside)

Facing (right side/upside)

Front (wrong side/reverse)

no. 2 one-piece side drape dress
see page 18 for instructions

no. 2 one-piece side drape dress

◆ **Required pattern pieces (side B)**

1 Bodice (align the pattern piece for the right front and back with that for the left front and back)

◆ **Sewing instructions**

1 Finish the neckline (see figure 1 on p. 19).
2 Finish the left armhole.
3 Sew the left side seam (see figure 3 on p. 19).
4 Sew from the right sleeve seam to the right side seam (see figure 4 on p. 19).
5 Fold and stitch the seam allowance on the sleeve hem.
6 Fold and stitch the seam allowance on the hem.

◆ **Widths and lengths used**

Fabric: lace
= W 1 m 40 cm
L 1 m 90 cm

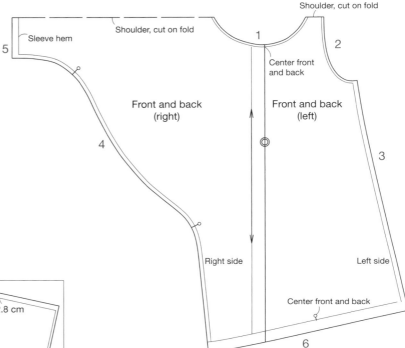

Cutting layout

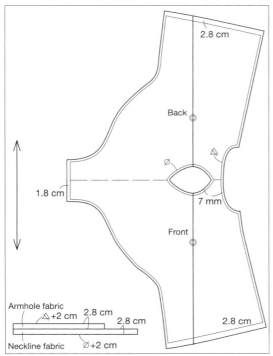

* Seam allowance is 1 cm, unless specified

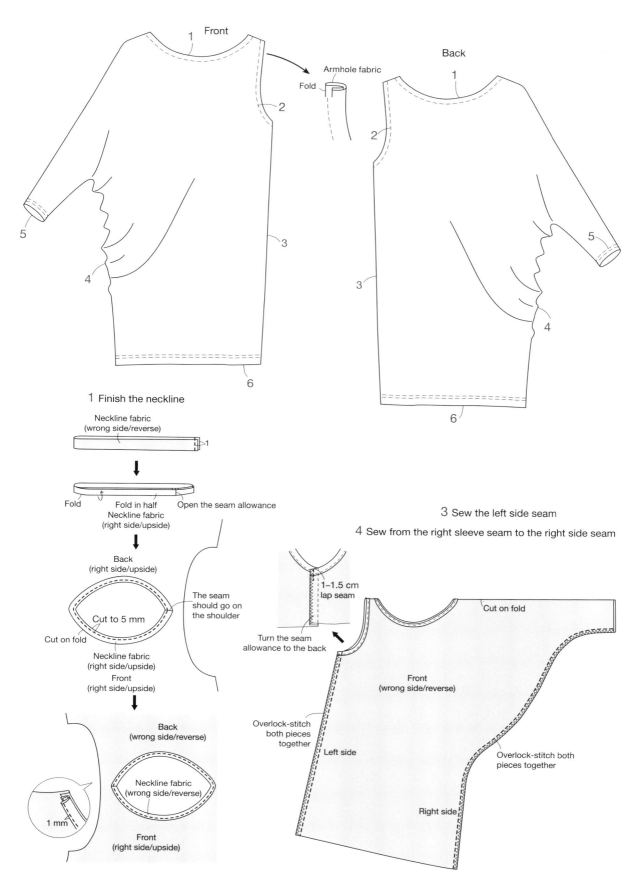

Front

1

Back

Armhole fabric

Fold

2

2

1

5

3

3

4

5

4

6

6

1 Finish the neckline

Neckline fabric
(wrong side/reverse)

1

Fold   Fold in half   Open the seam allowance
Neckline fabric
(right side/upside)

Back
(right side/upside)

Cut to 5 mm

Cut on fold

Neckline fabric
(right side/upside)

Front
(right side/upside)

The seam
should go on
the shoulder

Back
(wrong side/reverse)

Neckline fabric
(wrong side/reverse)

1 mm

Front
(right side/upside)

3 Sew the left side seam

4 Sew from the right sleeve seam to the right side seam

1–1.5 cm
lap seam

Turn the seam
allowance to the back

Cut on fold

Front
(wrong side/reverse)

Overlock-stitch
both pieces
together

Left side

Right side

Overlock-stitch both
pieces together

no. 3 three-piece cowl-neck top
+ no. 4 three-piece tucked-hip pants
see page 22, 25 for instructions

no. 3 three-piece cowl-neck top

◆ **Required pattern pieces (side A)**

1 Back
2 Front (align the top and hem)
3 Cuff

◆ **Sewing instructions**

* Attach fusible stay tape to the seam allowance on the back neckline.

1 Finish the back neckline (see figure 1 on p. 23).

2 Fold and stitch the seam allowance at the edge of the facing (see figure 2 on p. 24).

3 Sew from the shoulders to the sleeve caps (see figure 3 on p. 24).

4 Sew from the side seams to the sleeve seams.

5 Fold up the hem, and stitch.

6 Make the cuffs and attach them to the sleeve openings (see figure 6 on p. 24).

◆ **Widths and lengths used**

Fabric: stretch fabric/cotton jersey (plain knit)
= W 1 m 50 cm x L 2 m
Fusible stay tape (suitable for use with knitted fabric)
= W 7 mm x L 30 cm

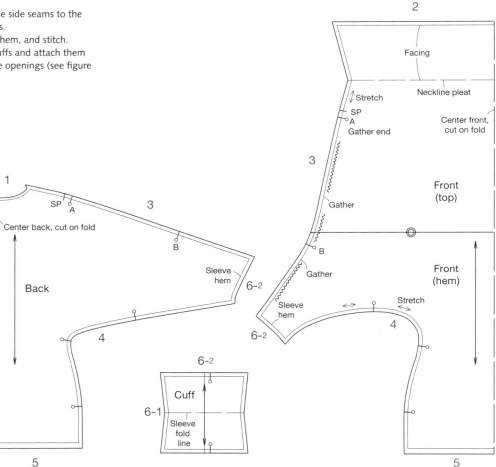

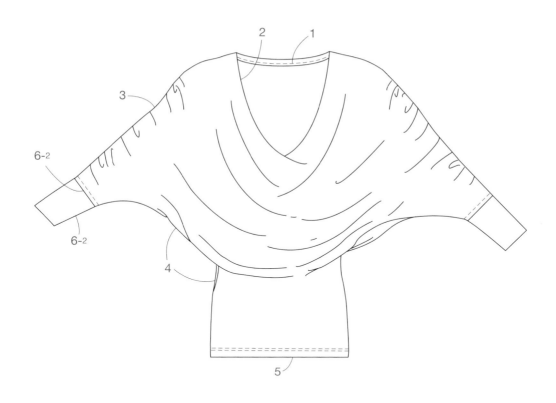

Cutting layout

Back

Cut on fold

1.5 cm

Back neckline binding (x 1)

2 cm

△ x 2 + 2

Front

Cuff

1.5 cm

5 mm

W = 1 m 50 cm

* Seam allowance is 1 cm, unless specified

1 Finish the back neckline

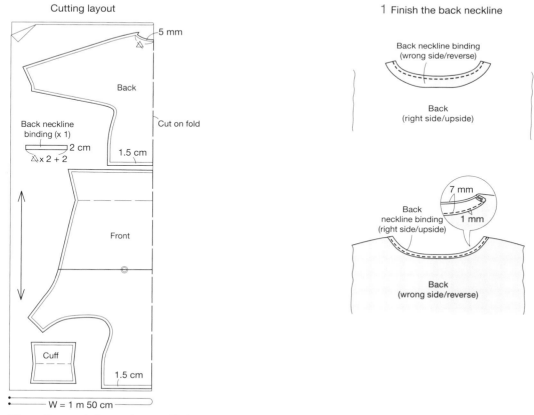

Back neckline binding
(wrong side/reverse)

Back
(right side/upside)

Back
neckline binding
(right side/upside)

7 mm

1 mm

Back
(wrong side/reverse)

2 Fold the edge of the facing and stitch

3 Sew from the shoulders to the sleeve caps

6 Make the cuffs and attach them to the sleeve openings

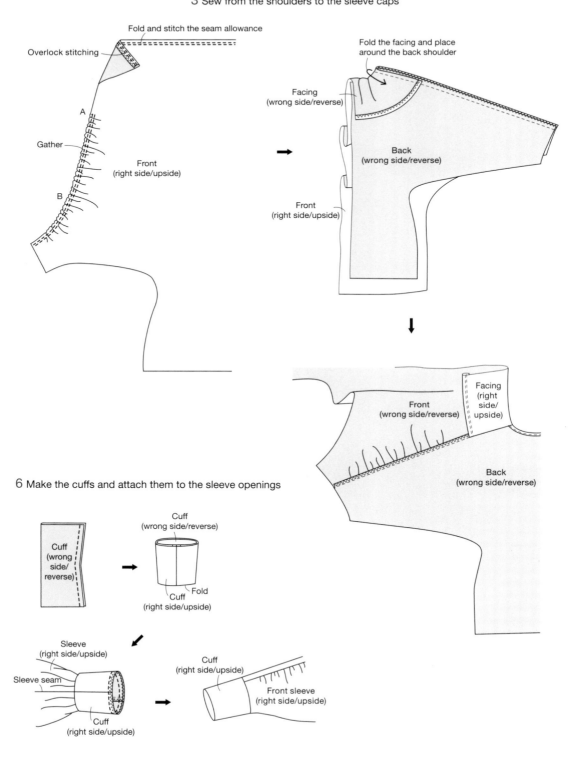

no. 4 three-piece tucked-hip pants

◆ Required pattern pieces (side A)

1 Front and back pants (align the top and hem)
2 Waistband

◆ Sewing instructions

* Attach fusible interfacing to the reverse at the point where the drawstring opening is located.
1 Sew the waist tucks (see figure 1 on p. 27).
2 Sew the inseams.
3 Sew the crotch seams (see figure 3 on p. 27).
4 Make the waistband (see figure 4 on p. 27).
5 Attach the waistband (see figure 5 on p. 27.
6 Finish the hem (see figure 6 on p. 27).
7 Pass the drawstring through the inside of the waistband.

◆ Widths and lengths used

Fabric: stretch fabric/cotton jersey (plain knit)
= W 1 m 50 cm
L 1 m 80 cm (S), 1 m 90 cm (M), 2 m (L), 2 m 10 cm (XL)
Adhesive interfacing (for use with knitted fabrics)
= Length to suit
Elastic tape = W 35 mm
Drawstring = W 1 cm L 1 m 45 cm

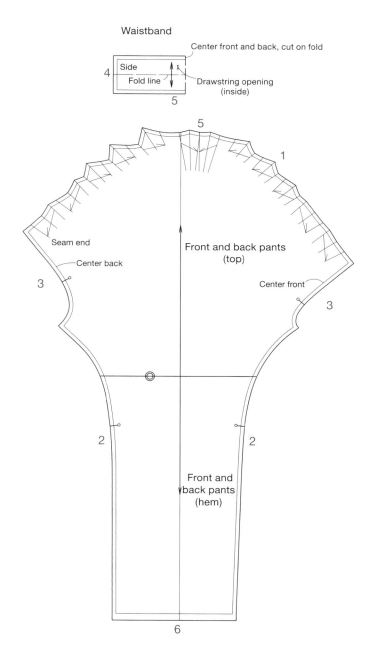

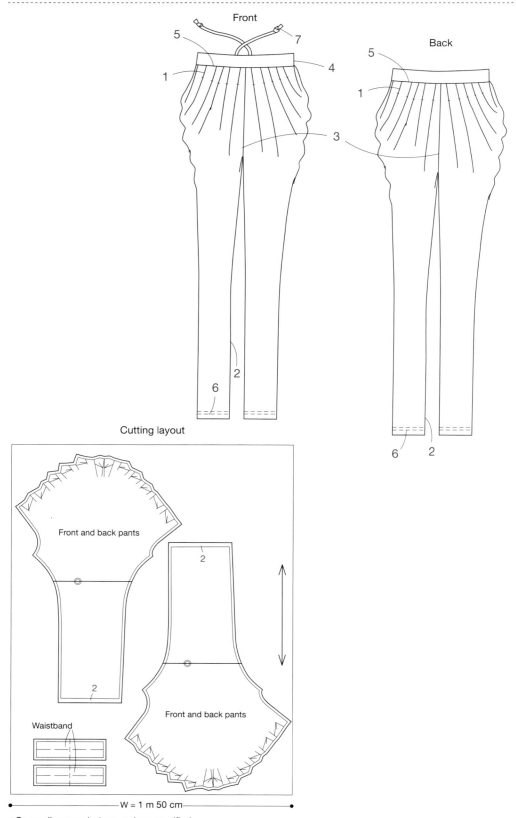

Front

Back

Cutting layout

Front and back pants

Front and back pants

Waistband

W = 1 m 50 cm

* Seam allowance is 1 cm, unless specified

1 Sew the waist tucks

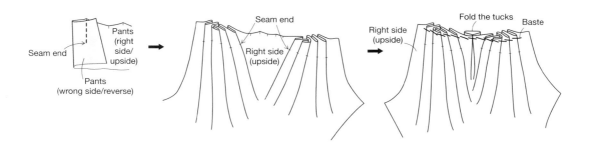

Seam end

Pants (right side/upside)

Seam end

Pants (wrong side/reverse)

Seam end

Right side (upside)

Fold the tucks

Baste

Right side (upside)

3 Sew the crotch seams

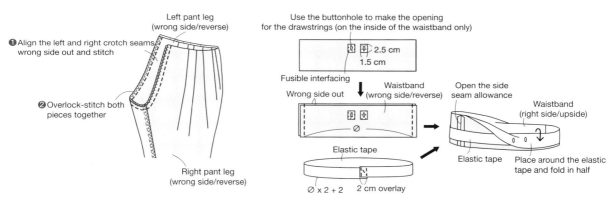

❶ Align the left and right crotch seams wrong side out and stitch

❷ Overlock-stitch both pieces together

Left pant leg (wrong side/reverse)

Right pant leg (wrong side/reverse)

4 Make the waistband

Use the buttonhole to make the opening for the drawstrings (on the inside of the waistband only)

2.5 cm
1.5 cm

Fusible interfacing

Wrong side out

Waistband (wrong side/reverse)

Open the side seam allowance

Waistband (right side/upside)

Elastic tape

∅ x 2 + 2

2 cm overlay

Elastic tape

Place around the elastic tape and fold in half

5 Attach the waistband

❶ Stretch all 3 pieces of fabric together, stitching as you go

❷ Overlock-stitch all 3 pieces together

Waistband (right side/upside, inside)

Cut on fold

Pants (right side/upside)

Center front

6 Finish the hem

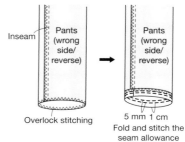

Inseam

Pants (wrong side/reverse)

Pants (wrong side/reverse)

Overlock stitching

5 mm 1 cm
Fold and stitch the seam allowance

no. 5 four-piece batwing bubble top
see page 32 for instructions

no. 6 two-piece asymmetrical wrap dress
see page 35 for instructions

no. 5 four-piece batwing bubble top

◆ **Required pattern pieces (side A)**

1 Back
2 Front (align the top and hem)

◆ **Sewing instructions**

1 Finish the slit at the shoulders with a threefold edge-stitched seam (see figure 1 on p. 33).
2 French-seam the shoulders (see figure 2 on p. 34).
3 Finish the sleeve hems with a threefold edge-stitched seam.
4 Finish the neckline with a threefold edge-stitched seam.
5 French-seam from A to B on the back bodice (see figure 5 on p. 34).
6 French-seam the center back. Finish the sleeve hems.
7 French-seam the center front.
8 Finish the hem with a threefold edge-stitched seam.
9 Fold the cuffs in and blind-stitch to hold in place (see figure 9 on p. 34).

◆ **Widths and lengths used**

Fabric: woven fabric/print
= W 1 m 10 cm x L 3 m

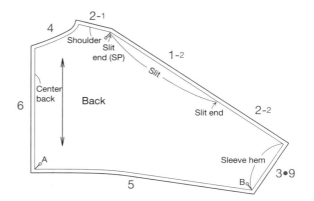

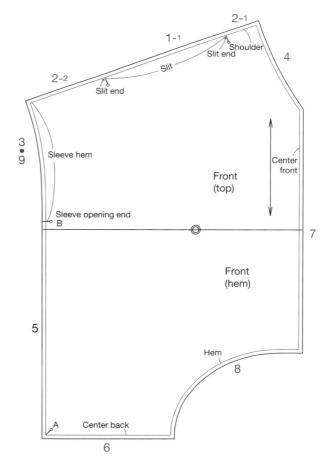

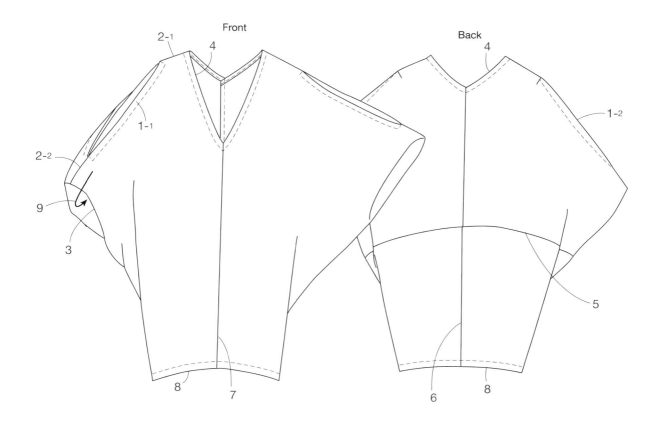

Front

Back

2-1
4
1-1
2-2
9
3
8
7

4
1-2
5
6
8

1 Finish the slit opening at the shoulders with a threefold edge-stitched seam

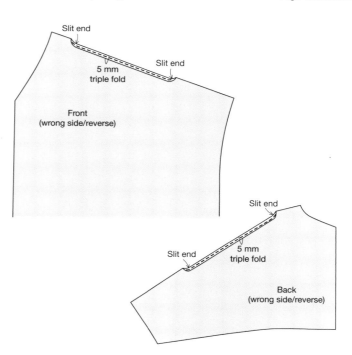

Slit end
5 mm
triple fold
Slit end

Front
(wrong side/reverse)

Slit end
5 mm
triple fold
Slit end

Back
(wrong side/reverse)

Cutting layout

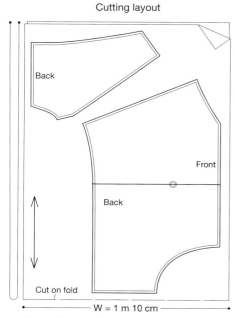

Back

Front

Back

Cut on fold

W = 1 m 10 cm

*Seam allowance is 1 cm, unless specified

2 French-seam the shoulders

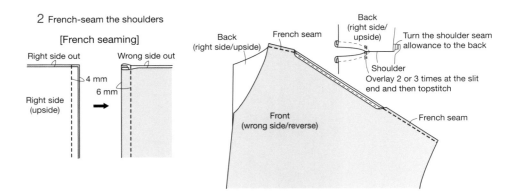

5 French-seam the back bodice from A to B

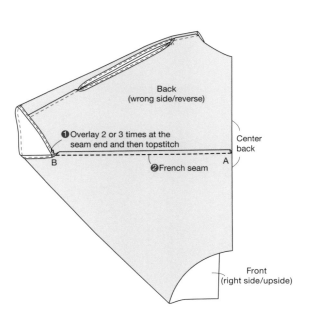

9 Fold the cuffs in and blind-stitch to hold in place

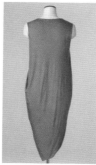

no. 6 two-piece asymmetrical wrap dress

◆ **Required pattern pieces (side B)**

1 Bodice (align the left back (top), left back (hem), right side (top), right side (hem), left front (top), and left front (hem))
2 Bodice facing (align the right and left)
3 Armhole fabric
4 Back neckline binding

◆ **Sewing instructions**

* Attach fusible stay tape to the seam allowance on the neckline and armholes.

1 Sew darts in the bodice facing and finish the right side (see figure 1 on p. 37).

2 Sew tucks in the front of the shoulders and right armhole, then fold two tucks in the top of the left side (front and back) and baste to secure them in place (see figure 2 on p. 37).

3 Sew the bodice facing to the bodice at the neckline (see figure 3 on p. 38).

4 Sew the triangle-shaped section of the bodice hem. Finish the hem and fold the hem facing, then fold the tucks in both sections of fabric together (see figure 4 on p. 38).

5 Sew the left side, and then fold the tucks in the left armhole (see figure 5 on p. 39).

6 Finish the back neckline with the back neckline binding.

7 Finish the armholes with the armhole bindings.

8 Sew the shoulders.

◆ **Widths and lengths used**

Fabric: stretch fabric/jersey (plain knit)
= W 150 cm
L 2 m 30 cm (S, M), 2 m 50 cm (L, XL)
Fusible stay tape
= W 8 mm x L 30 cm

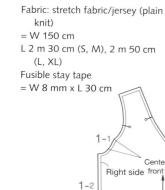

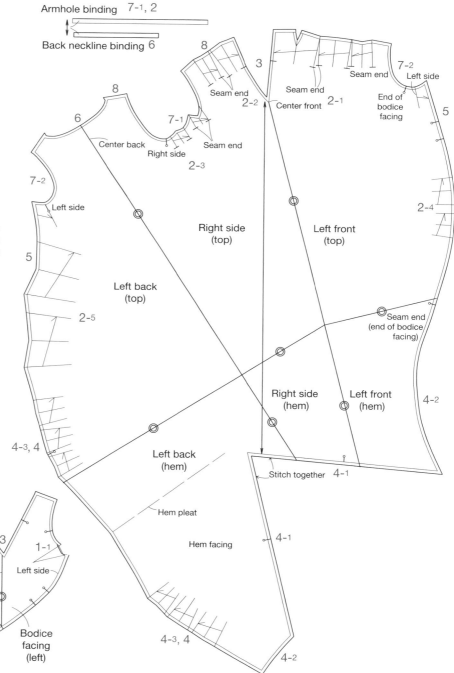

Armhole binding 7-1, 2

Back neckline binding 6

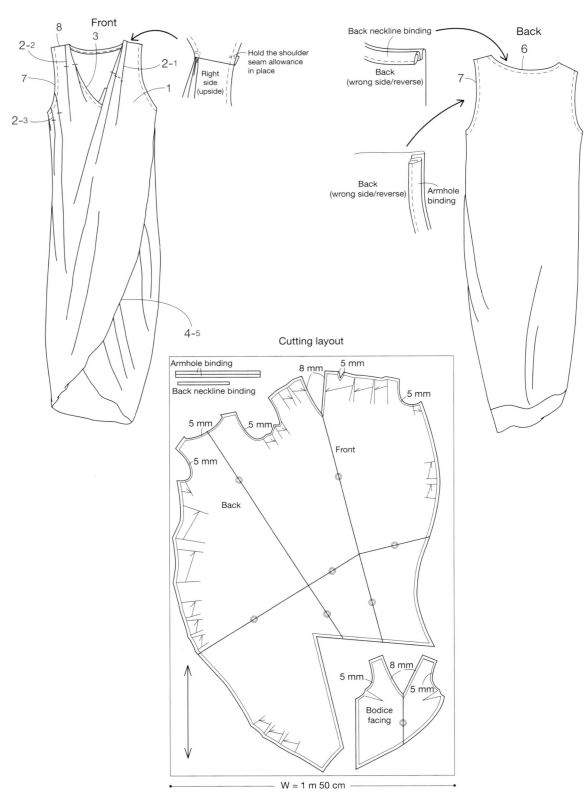

Front

8
3

2-2
2-1
7
1
2-3

Hold the shoulder
seam allowance
in place

Right
side
(upside)

4-5

Back neckline binding

Back
(wrong side/reverse)

Back

6

7

Back
(wrong side/reverse)

Armhole
binding

Cutting layout

Armhole binding

Back neckline binding

8 mm   5 mm

5 mm

5 mm   5 mm

Front

5 mm

5 mm

Back

5 mm   8 mm

Bodice
facing

5 mm

W = 1 m 50 cm

* Seam allowance is 1 cm, unless specified

1 Sew darts in the bodice facing and finish the right side

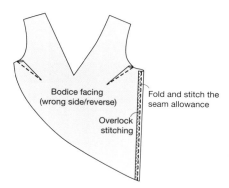

Bodice facing
(wrong side/reverse)

Fold and stitch the
seam allowance

Overlock
stitching

2 Sew tucks in the front shoulders and right armhole, then fold two tucks
   in the top of the left side (front and back) and baste in place

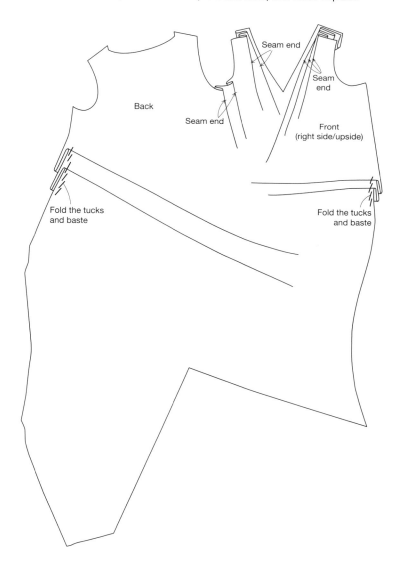

Back

Seam end

Seam end

Seam
end

Front
(right side/upside)

Fold the tucks
and baste

Fold the tucks
and baste

3 Sew the front neckline

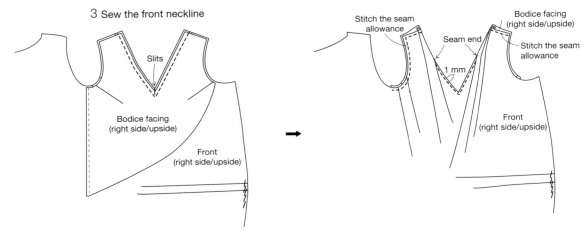

Slits

Bodice facing
(right side/upside)

Front
(right side/upside)

Stitch the seam
allowance

Seam end

Bodice facing
(right side/upside)

Stitch the seam
allowance

1 mm

Front
(right side/upside)

4 Stitch the triangle-shaped section on the bodice hem, and finish the hem.
Fold the hem facing and then fold both tucks together

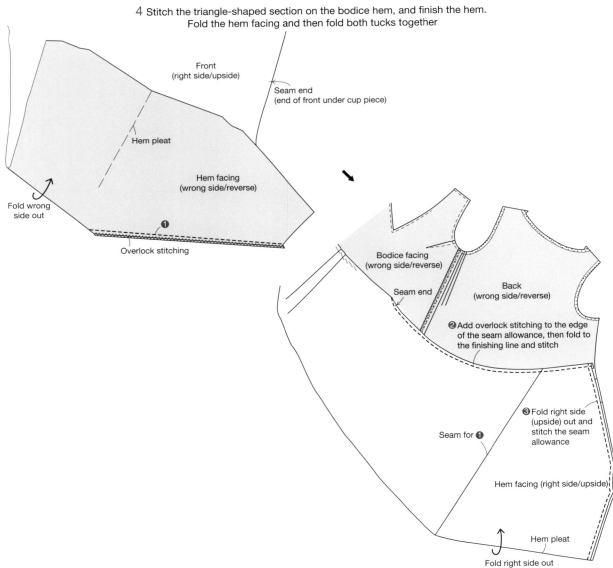

Front
(right side/upside)

Seam end
(end of front under cup piece)

Hem pleat

Hem facing
(wrong side/reverse)

Fold wrong
side out

Overlock stitching

❶

Bodice facing
(wrong side/reverse)

Seam end

Back
(wrong side/reverse)

❷Add overlock stitching to the edge
of the seam allowance, then fold to
the finishing line and stitch

❸Fold right side
(upside) out and
stitch the seam
allowance

Seam for ❶

Hem facing (right side/upside)

Hem pleat

Fold right side out

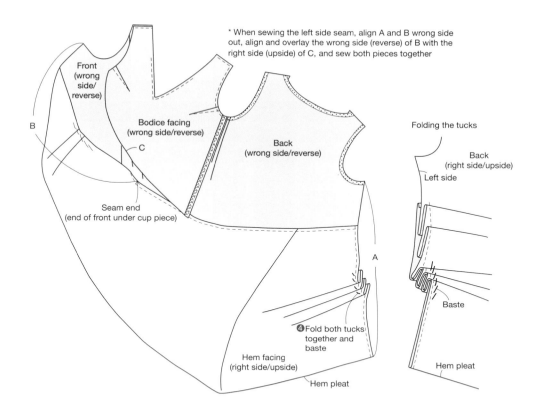

* When sewing the left side seam, align A and B wrong side out, align and overlay the wrong side (reverse) of B with the right side (upside) of C, and sew both pieces together

Front (wrong side/reverse)

B

Bodice facing (wrong side/reverse)

C

Back (wrong side/reverse)

Folding the tucks

Back (right side/upside)

Left side

Seam end (end of front under cup piece)

A

Baste

❹ Fold both tucks together and baste

Hem facing (right side/upside)

Hem pleat

Hem pleat

5 Sew the left side, and then fold the tucks in the left armhole

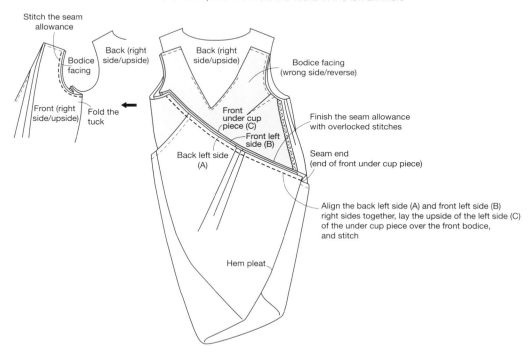

Stitch the seam allowance

Bodice facing

Back (right side/upside)

Back (right side/upside)

Bodice facing (wrong side/reverse)

Front (right side/upside)

Fold the tuck

Front under cup piece (C)

Front left side (B)

Back left side (A)

Finish the seam allowance with overlocked stitches

Seam end (end of front under cup piece)

Align the back left side (A) and front left side (B) right sides together, lay the upside of the left side (C) of the under cup piece over the front bodice, and stitch

Hem pleat

no. 7 two-piece v-neck blouse
+ no. 8 three-piece tuck drape shorts
see page 42, 44 for instructions

no. 7 two-piece v-neck blouse

◆ **Required pattern pieces (side B)**

1 Bodice (align the back and front)
2 Cuff

◆ **Sewing instructions**

* Attach fusible stay tape to the
  seam allowance on the neckline.
1 Finish the neckline.
2 Sew the center front.
3 Fold and arrange the tucks in
  the center front (see figure 3
  on p. 43).
4 Sew from the sleeve seams to the
  side seams.
5 Finish the hem with a threefold
  edge-stitched seam.
6 Gather the sleeve openings and
  attach the cuffs.

◆ **Widths and lengths used**

Fabric: linen
= W 1 m 35 cm
L 1 m 80 cm
Fusible stay tape
= W 7 mm, length to suit

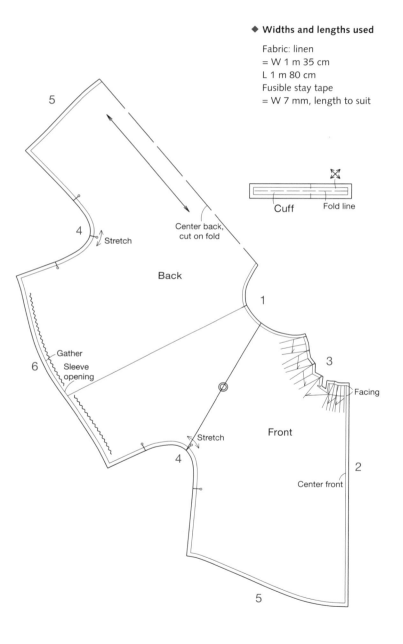

Cuff
Fold line

5

Center back,
cut on fold

Back

1

4 Stretch

Gather
Sleeve
opening
6

3

Facing

Front

4 Stretch

2

Center front

5

Cutting layout

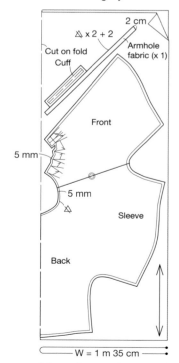

2 cm
△ x 2 + 2
Cut on fold
Cuff
Armhole
fabric (x 1)

Front

5 mm

5 mm
△
Sleeve

Back

W = 1 m 35 cm

* Seam allowance is 1 cm, unless specified

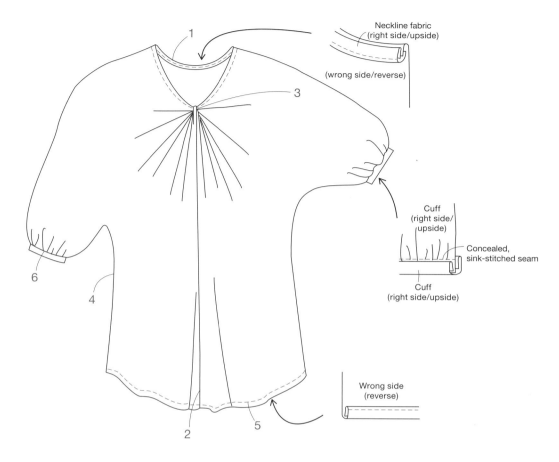

Neckline fabric
(right side/upside)

(wrong side/reverse)

Cuff
(right side/upside)

Concealed,
sink-stitched seam

Cuff
(right side/upside)

Wrong side
(reverse)

3 Fold and arrange the tucks in the center front

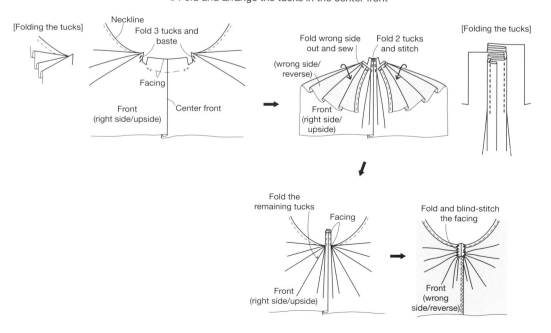

[Folding the tucks]

Neckline
Fold 3 tucks and
baste

Facing

Front
(right side/upside)

Center front

Fold wrong side
out and sew

(wrong side/
reverse)

Fold 2 tucks
and stitch

Front
(right side/
upside)

[Folding the tucks]

Fold the
remaining tucks

Facing

Front
(right side/upside)

Fold and blind-stitch
the facing

Front
(wrong
side/reverse)

no. 8 three-piece tuck drape shorts

◆ **Required pattern pieces (side C)**

1 Front and back pants (align the back and front)
2 Cuff
3 Waistband (elastic tape)

◆ **Sewing instructions**

1 Fold the tucks in the waist, but leave the center front and back sections untucked for the moment (see figure 1 on p. 45).
2 Sew the sides.
3 Sew the inseams.
4 Sew the cuff seams and attach to the hem of the shorts. Thread the cuffs with the elastic tape, fold them inside, and then topstitch (see figure 4 on p. 45).
5 Sew the crotch seams.
6 Sew the side of the waistband.
7 Fold the tucks in the center front and center back, and then attach the waistband. Lay the elastic-tape waistband over the waist seam allowance of the shorts. Aligning the notches, stretch the waistband and double-stitch in place.

◆ **Widths and lengths used**

Fabric: doubleknit (double rib)
= W 150 cm
L 1 m 80 cm
Elastic tape (for waistband)
= W 8 cm x L 70 cm (S, M), 80 cm (L, XL)
Elastic tape (for cuffs)
= W 3 cm x L 1 m 20 cm (S, M), 1 m 40 cm (L, XL)

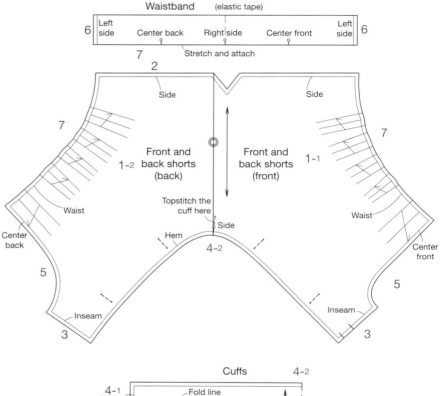

Waistband (elastic tape)

6 | Left side | Center back | Right side | Center front | Left side | 6
7 — Stretch and attach

2 — Side — Side

Front and back shorts (back) 1-2 | 1-1 Front and back shorts (front)

7 — Waist — Center back — 5 — Inseam — 3

Topstitch the cuff here — Side — Hem — 4-2

7 — Waist — Center front — 5 — Inseam — 3

Cuffs 4-2

4-1 Inseam — Fold line — Side

Cutting layout

Cuff

Front and back shorts (back) — (front)

Cut on fold

— W = 1 m 50 cm —

*Seam allowance is 1 cm, unless specified

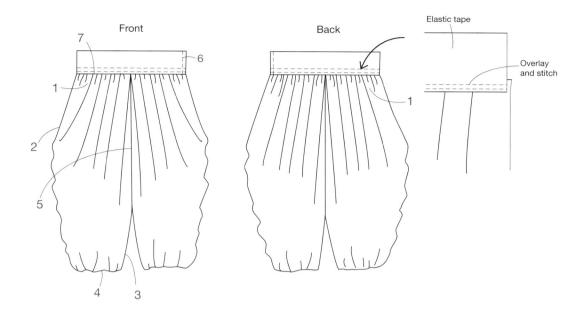

Front

Back

Elastic tape

Overlay and stitch

7
6
1
2
5
4
3

1 Fold the tucks in the waist, but leave the center front and back sections untucked for the moment

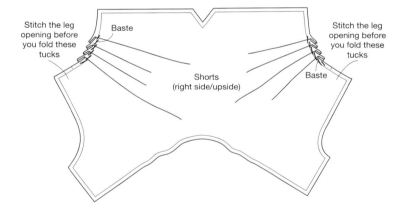

Stitch the leg opening before you fold these tucks

Baste

Stitch the leg opening before you fold these tucks

Baste

Shorts (right side/upside)

4 Sew the cuff seams and attach to the hem of the shorts

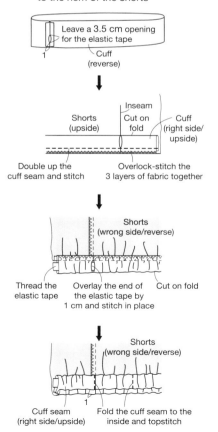

Leave a 3.5 cm opening for the elastic tape

1

Cuff (reverse)

Shorts (upside)

Inseam
Cut on fold

Cuff (right side/ upside)

Double up the cuff seam and stitch

Overlock-stitch the 3 layers of fabric together

Shorts (wrong side/reverse)

Thread the elastic tape

Overlay the end of the elastic tape by 1 cm and stitch in place

Cut on fold

Shorts (wrong side/reverse)

Cuff seam (right side/upside)

1

Fold the cuff seam to the inside and topstitch

no. 9 three-piece twist gather drape dress
see page 50 for instructions

no. 10 three-piece tuck drape skirt
see page 53 for instructions

no. 9 three-piece twist gather drape dress

◆ **Required pattern pieces (side B)**

1 Front (align the top right, right hem, top left, and left hem)
2 Back (align the top right, right hem, top left, and left hem)
3 Sleeve

◆ **Sewing instructions**

1 Finish the hem (see figure 1 on p. 51).
2 Gather the sides at both front and back and fold the tucks (see figure 2 on p. 52).
3 Sew the sides (see figure 3 on p. 52).
4 Sew the shoulders.
5 Finish the neckline with the neckline fabric.
6 Make the sleeves (see figure 6 on p. 52).
7 Attach the sleeves.

◆ **Widths and lengths used**

Fabric: stretch fabric/jersey (plain knit)
= W 1 m 50 cm x L 2 m 40 cm

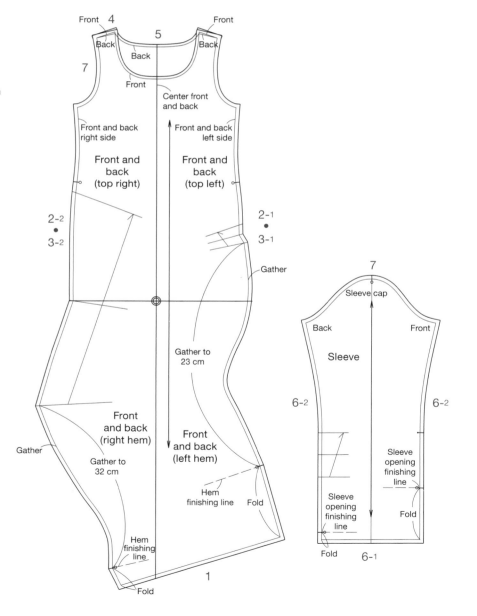

Front

Back

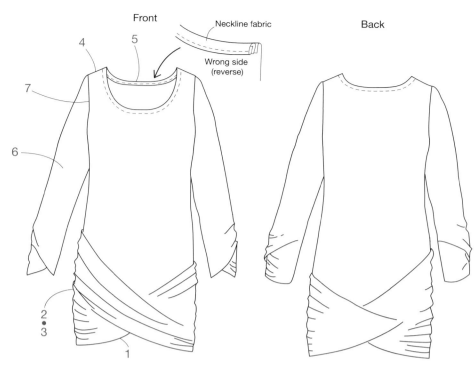

Neckline fabric

Wrong side (reverse)

4
5
7
6
2
3
1

Cutting layout

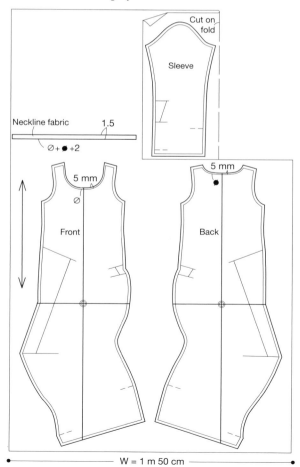

Cut on fold

Sleeve

Neckline fabric   1.5

∅ + ● +2

5 mm

∅

Front

5 mm

Back

W = 1 m 50 cm

*Seam allowance is 1 cm, unless specified

1 Finish the hem

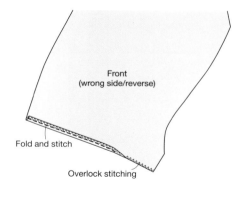

Front
(wrong side/reverse)

Fold and stitch

Overlock stitching

2 Gather the sides and fold the tucks

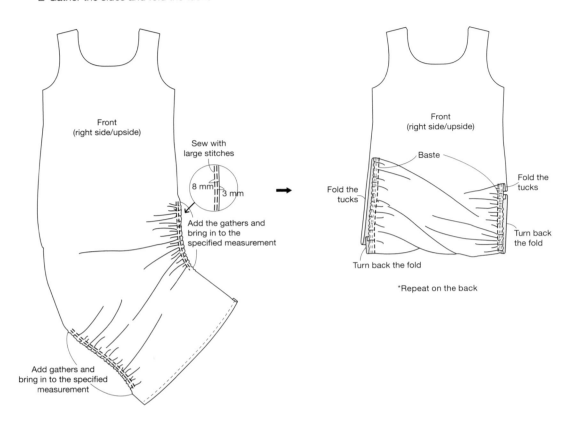

Front
(right side/upside)

Sew with
large stitches

8 mm   3 mm

Add the gathers and
bring in to the
specified measurement

Add gathers and
bring in to the specified
measurement

Front
(right side/upside)

Baste

Fold the
tucks

Fold the
tucks

Turn back
the fold

Turn back the fold

*Repeat on the back

3 Sew the sides   6 Make the sleeves

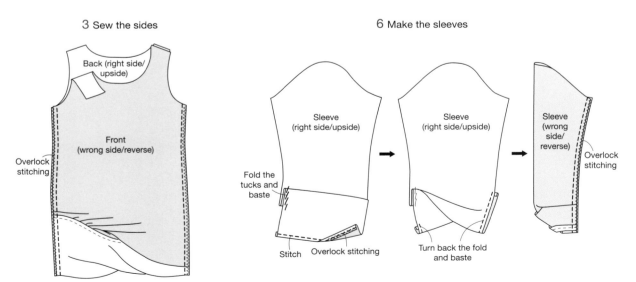

Back (right side/
upside)

Front
(wrong side/reverse)

Overlock
stitching

Sleeve
(right side/upside)

Sleeve
(right side/upside)

Sleeve
(wrong
side/
reverse)

Overlock
stitching

Fold the
tucks and
baste

Stitch   Overlock stitching

Turn back the fold
and baste

no. 10 three-piece tuck drape skirt

◆ **Required pattern pieces (side C)**

1 Front
2 Back
3 Panel (align the top, right hem, and left hem)
4 Waistband (elastic tape)

◆ **Sewing instructions**

1 Sew the sides of the skirt. Lay the front over the back and stitch in place.
2 Finish the hem of the panel (see figure 2 on p. 55).
3 Fold the tucks in the panel fabric (see figure 3 on p. 55).
4 Lay the panel over the skirt and baste to the waist.
5 Sew the two ends of the waistband together to form a loop.
6 Attach the waistband. Aligning the notches on the skirt and waistband, stretch the waistband in line with the skirt, stitching as you go.

◆ **Widths and lengths used**

Fabric A: stretch fabric/doubleknit (double rib)
  = W 1 m 50 cm x L 1 m 40 cm
Fabric B: synthetic leather
  = W 1 m 10 cm x L 50 cm
Elastic (for waistband) = W 6 cm x L 68 cm (S), 72 cm (M), 76 cm (L), 80 cm (XL)

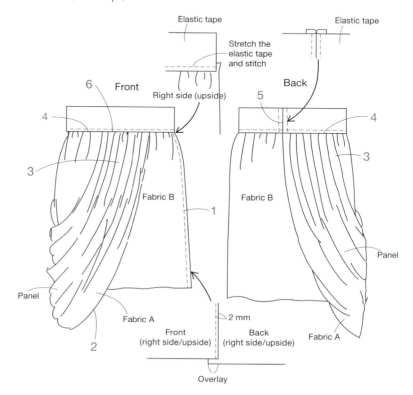

Cutting layout

Fabric B

Front

Back

W = 1 m 10 cm

Fabric A

Panel (top)

(Left hem)

(Right hem)

W = 1 m 50 cm

* Seam allowance is 1 cm, unless specified

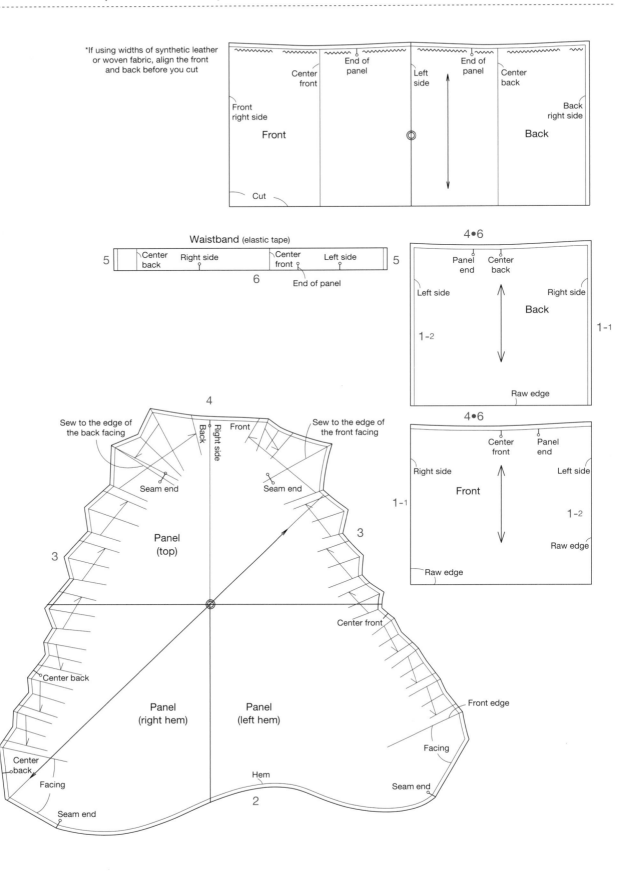

*If using widths of synthetic leather or woven fabric, align the front and back before you cut

Center front
End of panel
Left side
End of panel
Center back

Front right side

Front

Back right side

Back

Cut

Waistband (elastic tape)

5

Center back

Right side

Center front

Left side

5

6

End of panel

4•6

Panel end
Center back

Left side

Right side

Back

1-2

1-1

Raw edge

4•6

Center front
Panel end

Right side

Left side

1-1

Front

1-2

Raw edge

Raw edge

Sew to the edge of the back facing

4

Right side
Back

Front

Sew to the edge of the front facing

Seam end

Seam end

Panel (top)

3

3

Center front

Center back

Panel (right hem)

Panel (left hem)

Front edge

Facing

Center back

Facing

Hem

Seam end

Seam end

2

2 Finish the hem of the panel

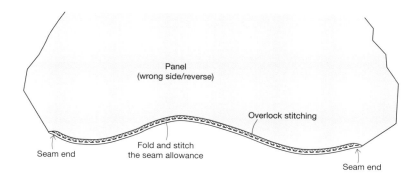

Panel
(wrong side/reverse)

Overlock stitching

Seam end

Fold and stitch
the seam allowance

Seam end

3 Fold the tucks in the panel

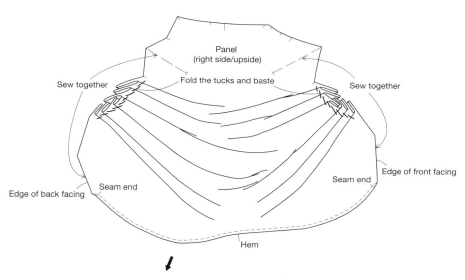

Sew together

Panel
(right side/upside)

Fold the tucks and baste

Sew together

Edge of back facing

Seam end

Seam end

Edge of front facing

Hem

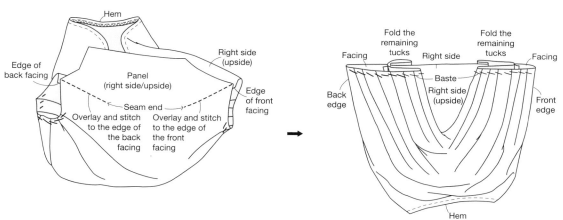

Hem

Edge of
back facing

Panel
(right side/upside)

Seam end

Overlay and stitch
to the edge of
the back
facing

Overlay and stitch
to the edge of
the front
facing

Right side
(upside)

Edge
of front
facing

Facing

Fold the
remaining
tucks

Right side

Fold the
remaining
tucks

Facing

Back
edge

Baste

Right side
(upside)

Front
edge

Hem

no. 11 three-piece sundress
see page 58 for instructions

no. 11 three-piece sundress

◆ Sewing instructions

1 Sew the center fronts of the bodice and lining up to the notches.

2 On the bodice and lining, sew together the top back edges from the armhole seam ends to the center back. Attach the top edge of the lining to the bodice (see figure 2 on p. 60).

3 Sew the tucks in the center front (see figure 3 on p. 60).

4 Finish the seam allowance above the seam end on the ribbon with a threefold edge-stitched seam.

5 Sew together the bodice and ribbon (see figure 5 on p. 61).

6 Sew from the tuck seam end on the bodice to the seam end on the ribbon (see figure 6 on p. 61).

7 Sew down from the ends of the openings on the center back of the bodice and lining (see figure 7 on p. 61).

8 Attach an invisible zipper to the center back (see figure 8 on p. 61).

9 Finish the hems on the bodice and lining with threefold edge-stitched seams.

10 Tie the left and right ribbons together into a single bow at a position around the tuck seam ends.

◆ Required pattern pieces (side C)

1 Bodice
2 Lining
3 Ribbon

◆ Widths and lengths used

Fabric: woven fabric/print
= W 1 m 10 cm x L 2 m 30 cm
Lining: polyester chiffon
= W 1 m 10 cm x L 2 m
1 x 56 cm invisible zipper

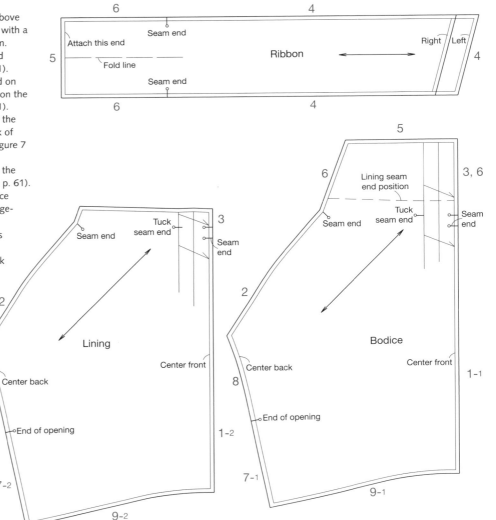

Front

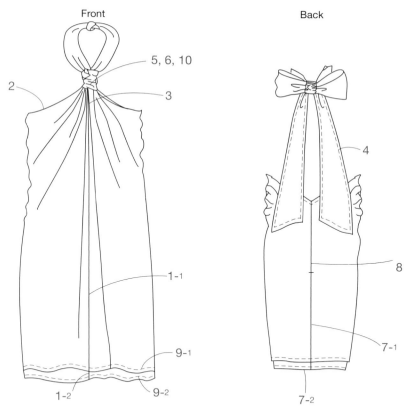

5, 6, 10

2

3

1-1

9-1

1-2

9-2

Back

4

8

7-1

7-2

Cutting layout

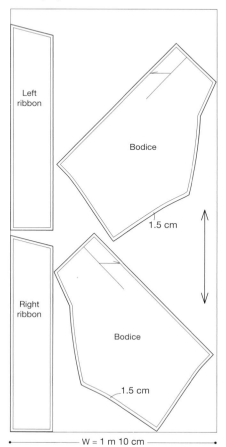

Left ribbon

Bodice

1.5 cm

Right ribbon

Bodice

1.5 cm

W = 1 m 10 cm

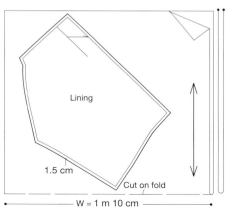

Lining

1.5 cm

Cut on fold

W = 1 m 10 cm

* Seam allowance is 1 cm, unless specified

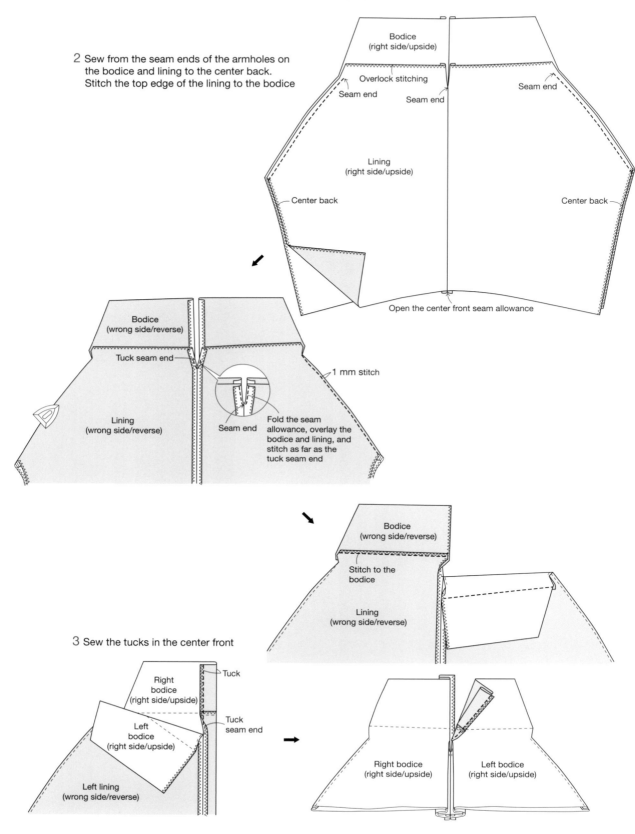

2 Sew from the seam ends of the armholes on the bodice and lining to the center back. Stitch the top edge of the lining to the bodice

Bodice (right side/upside)

Overlock stitching

Seam end

Seam end

Seam end

Lining (right side/upside)

Center back

Center back

Open the center front seam allowance

Bodice (wrong side/reverse)

Tuck seam end

1 mm stitch

Lining (wrong side/reverse)

Seam end

Fold the seam allowance, overlay the bodice and lining, and stitch as far as the tuck seam end

Bodice (wrong side/reverse)

Stitch to the bodice

Lining (wrong side/reverse)

3 Sew the tucks in the center front

Tuck

Right bodice (right side/upside)

Tuck seam end

Left bodice (right side/upside)

Left lining (wrong side/reverse)

Right bodice (right side/upside)

Left bodice (right side/upside)

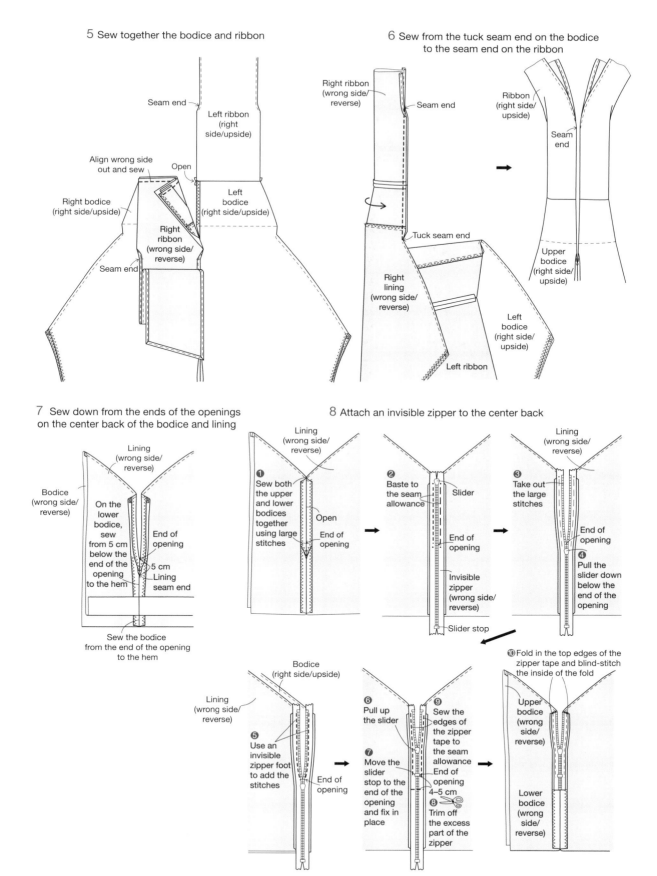

5 Sew together the bodice and ribbon

Seam end

Left ribbon (right side/upside)

Align wrong side out and sew

Open

Left bodice (right side/upside)

Right bodice (right side/upside)

Right ribbon (wrong side/reverse)

Seam end

6 Sew from the tuck seam end on the bodice to the seam end on the ribbon

Right ribbon (wrong side/reverse)

Seam end

Ribbon (right side/upside)

Seam end

Tuck seam end

Right lining (wrong side/reverse)

Upper bodice (right side/upside)

Left bodice (right side/upside)

Left ribbon

7 Sew down from the ends of the openings on the center back of the bodice and lining

Lining (wrong side/reverse)

Bodice (wrong side/reverse)

On the lower bodice, sew from 5 cm below the end of the opening to the hem

End of opening

5 cm

Lining seam end

Sew the bodice from the end of the opening to the hem

8 Attach an invisible zipper to the center back

Lining (wrong side/reverse)

❶ Sew both the upper and lower bodices together using large stitches

Open

End of opening

❷ Baste to the seam allowance

Slider

End of opening

Invisible zipper (wrong side/reverse)

Slider stop

Lining (wrong side/reverse)

❸ Take out the large stitches

End of opening

❹ Pull the slider down below the end of the opening

Bodice (right side/upside)

Lining (wrong side/reverse)

❺ Use an invisible zipper foot to add the stitches

End of opening

❻ Pull up the slider

❼ Move the slider stop to the end of the opening and fix in place

❽ Trim off the excess part of the zipper

❾ Sew the edges of the zipper tape to the seam allowance

End of opening

4–5 cm

❿ Fold in the top edges of the zipper tape and blind-stitch the inside of the fold

Upper bodice (wrong side/reverse)

Lower bodice (wrong side/reverse)

no. 12 three-piece gather drape wrap dress
see page 64 for instructions

no. 12 three-piece gather drape wrap dress

◆ **Required pattern pieces (side D)**

1 Bodice (align the back (top), back (hem), front right (top), and front right (hem))
2 Front left
3 Sleeve

◆ **Sewing instructions**

1 Fold and stitch the hem on the back, front right bodice, bow, and front left bodice.
2 Sew the shoulders (see figure 2 on p. 66).
3 Fold and stitch the seam allowance on the neckline (see figure 3 on p. 66).
4 Gather the left side of the back and sew to the front left bodice (see figure 4 on p. 66).
5 Fold the tucks in the left side of the panel, add the gathers, and stitch onto the left side of the bodice (see figure 5 on p. 67).
6 Stitch the front left edge onto the right side (see figure 6 on p. 67).

7 Fold and stitch the seam allowances on the sleeve seams and sleeve hems (see figure 7 on p. 67).
8 Attach the sleeves. Finish, leaving the under-sleeve seams open.

◆ **Widths and lengths used**

Fabric: stretch fabric/jersey (plain knit)
= W 1 m 55 cm x L 1 m 90 cm

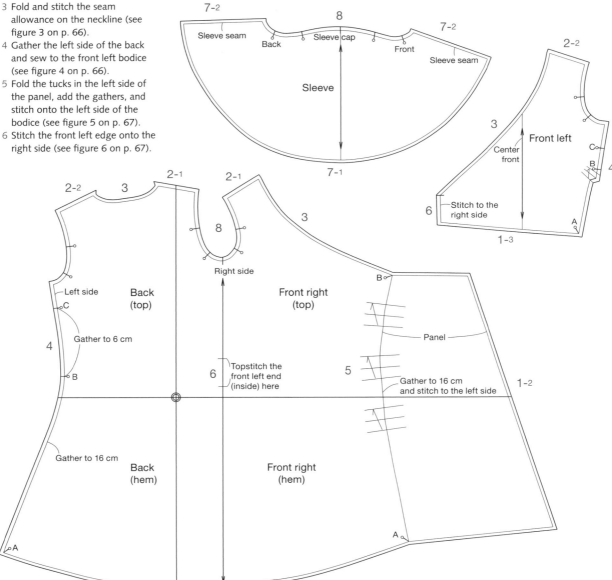

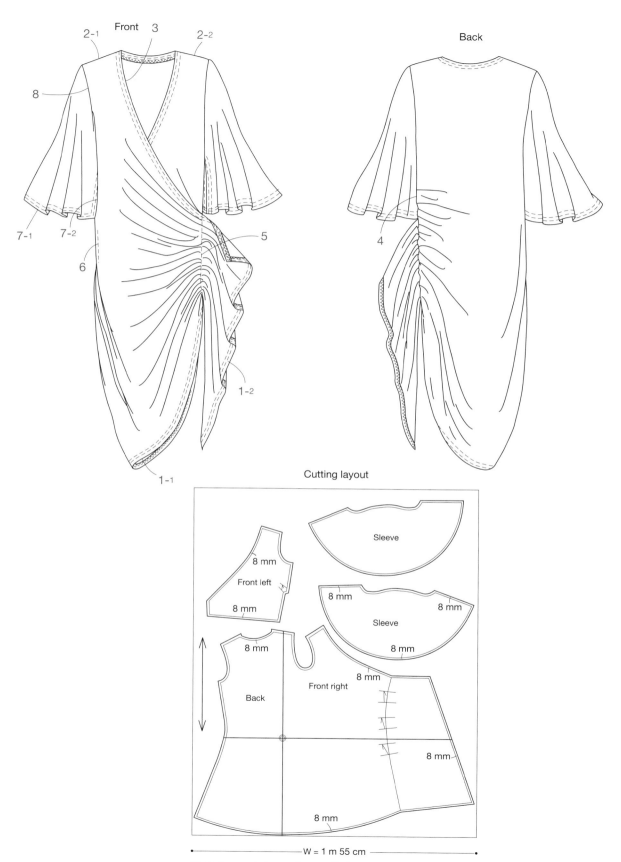

Front

2-1 3 2-2

8

7-1 7-2

6

5

1-2

1-1

Back

4

Cutting layout

Sleeve

8 mm

Front left

8 mm

8 mm

Sleeve

8 mm

8 mm

8 mm

Back

Front right

8 mm

8 mm

8 mm

— W = 1 m 55 cm —

Seam allowance is 1 cm, unless specified

2 Sew the shoulders

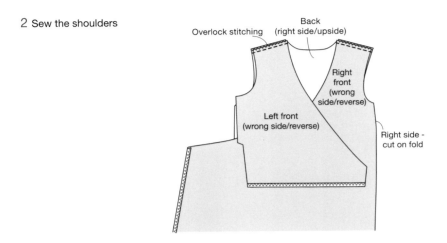

3 Fold and stitch the seam allowance on the neckline

4 Gather the back left side and sew to the front left bodice

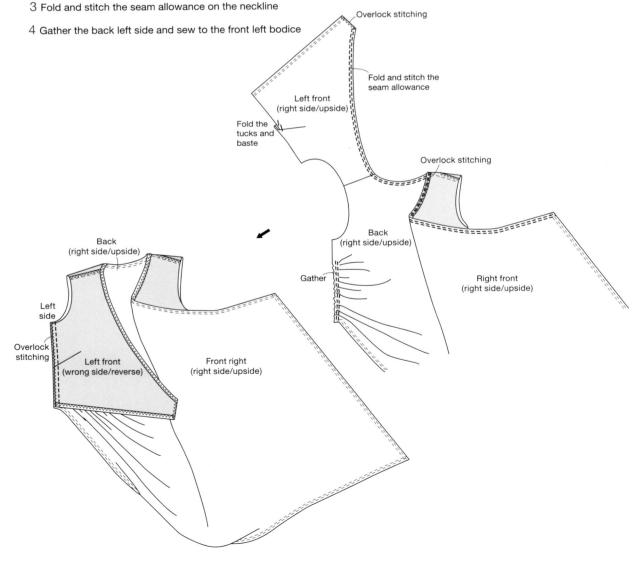

5 Fold the tucks in the left side of the panel, add the gathers, and stitch onto the left side of the bodice

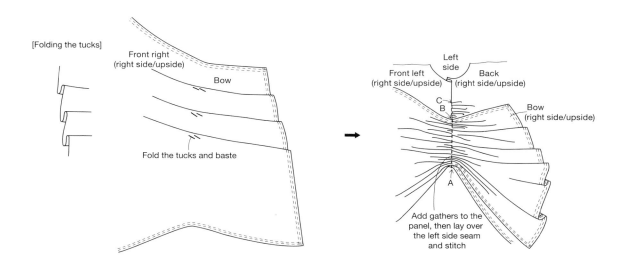

[Folding the tucks]

Front right
(right side/upside)

Bow

Fold the tucks and baste

Left side

Front left
(right side/upside)

Back
(right side/upside)

C
B

Bow
(right side/upside)

A

Add gathers to the
panel, then lay over
the left side seam
and stitch

6 Stitch the front left edge onto the right side

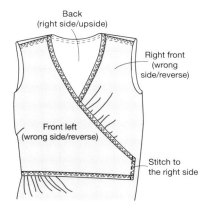

Back
(right side/upside)

Right front
(wrong side/reverse)

Front left
(wrong side/reverse)

Stitch to
the right side

7 Fold and stitch the seam allowances on the sleeve seams and sleeve hems

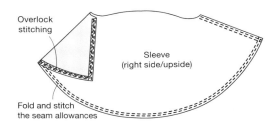

Overlock
stitching

Sleeve
(right side/upside)

Fold and stitch
the seam allowances

no. 13 one-piece boatneck tunic
see page 70 for instructions

no. 13 one-piece boatneck tunic

◆ **Required pattern pieces (side D)**

1 Front and back

◆ **Sewing instructions**

1 Bind the neckline.
2 Sew from the sides to the sleeve
   seams (see figure 2 on p. 71).
3 Fold and stitch the seam
   allowance on the sleeve hems.
4 Fold and stitch the seam
   allowance on the hem.

◆ **Widths and lengths used**

   Fabric: lace
   = W 1 m 40 cm x L = 1 m 60 cm

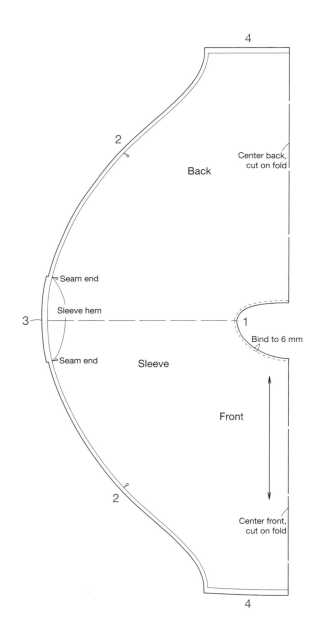

Cutting layout

Binding fabric

2.5 cm   1.5 cm

Cut on fold

Back

1.5 cm

0

Front

1.5 cm

W = 1 m 40 cm

*Seam allowance is 1 cm, unless specified

4

Center back, cut on fold

Back

2

Seam end

Sleeve hem

3

Seam end

Sleeve

1

Bind to 6 mm

Front

2

Center front, cut on fold

4

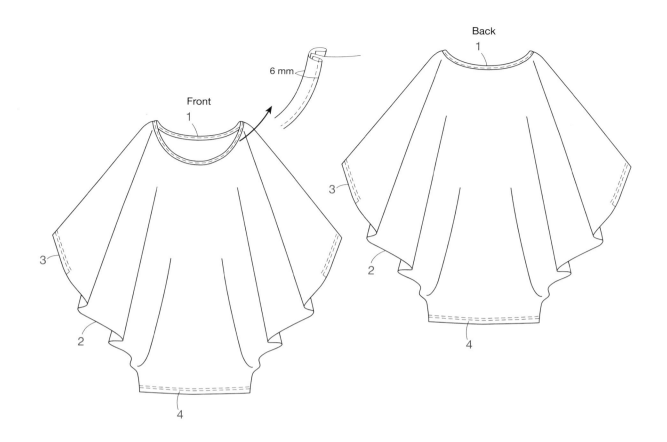

Front
1

6 mm

Back
1

3

2

3

2

4

4

2 Sew from the sides to the sleeve seams

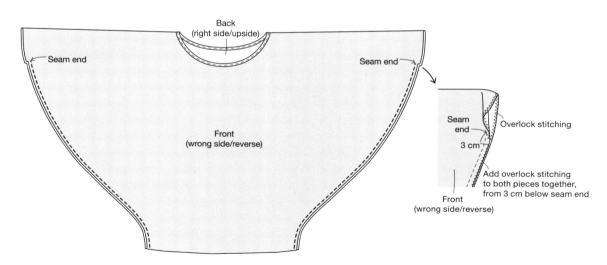

Back
(right side/upside)

Seam end

Seam end

Front
(wrong side/reverse)

Seam
end

Overlock stitching

3 cm

Add overlock stitching
to both pieces together,
from 3 cm below seam end

Front
(wrong side/reverse)

no. 14 eight-piece twist collar tuck drape dress
see page 74 for instructions

no. 14 eight-piece twist collar tuck drape dress

◆ **Required pattern pieces (side D)**

1 Back
2 Front right (align the side and center)
3 Front left
4 Collar (align the front and back)

5 Back lining
6 Front lining
7 Back armhole facing
8 Front armhole facing

◆ **Sewing instructions**

* Attach fusible interfacing to the front and back armhole facings.
1 Sew the center back and fold the tucks (see figure 1 on p. 77).
2 Sew together the left and right sides of the bodice front, and then fold the tucks (see figure 2 on p. 77).
3 Sew the sides.
4 Finish the hem with a threefold edge-stitched seam.
5 Sew the lining pieces together. Sew the tucks in the center back and then fold the tucks in the front. Sew the seams in the sides with 3 mm of fullness. Finish the hem with a threefold edge-stitched seam.
6 Sew the sides of the armhole facing and attach to the lining.
7 Sew the armholes.
8 Make the collar (see figure 8 on p. 77).
9 Attach the collar.

◆ **Widths and lengths used**

Fabric: stretch fabric/matte jersey (plain knit)
= W 135 cm x L 2 m 80 cm
Lining
= W 90 cm x L 1 m 70 cm (S, M),
   1 m 80 cm (L, XL)
Fusible interfacing
= W 90 cm x L 30 cm

Cutting layout

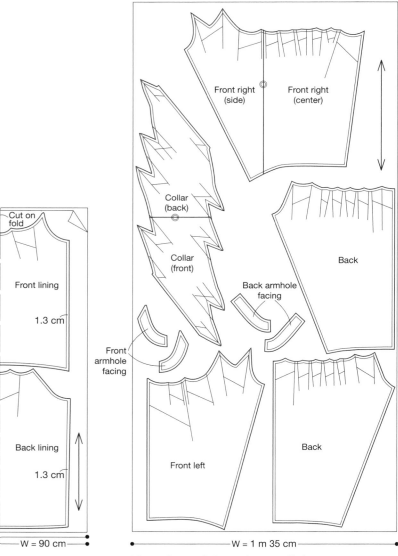

* Seam allowance is 1 cm, unlesss specified

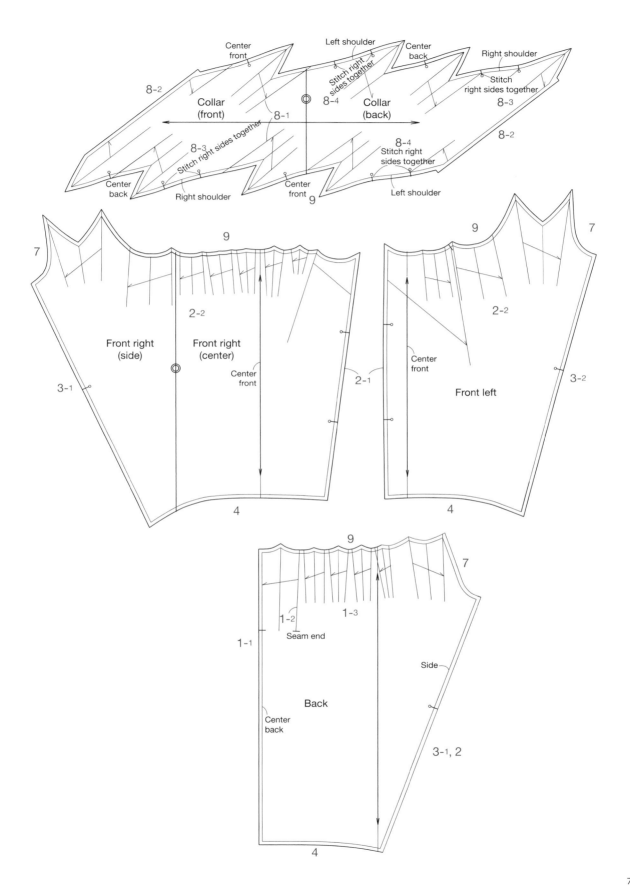

Center
front

Left shoulder

Center
back

Right shoulder

8-2

Collar
(front)

8-1

8-4

Collar
(back)

Stitch right
sides together

Stitch
right sides together

8-3

8-2

Stitch right sides together

8-3

Stitch right sides together

8-4

Stitch right
sides together

Center
back

Right shoulder

Center
front

9

Left shoulder

7

9

7

9

7

Front right
(side)

Front right
(center)

Center
front

2-2

2-2

Center
front

2-1

Front left

3-1

3-2

4

4

9

7

1-2

1-3

1-1

Seam end

Side

Back

Center
back

3-1, 2

4

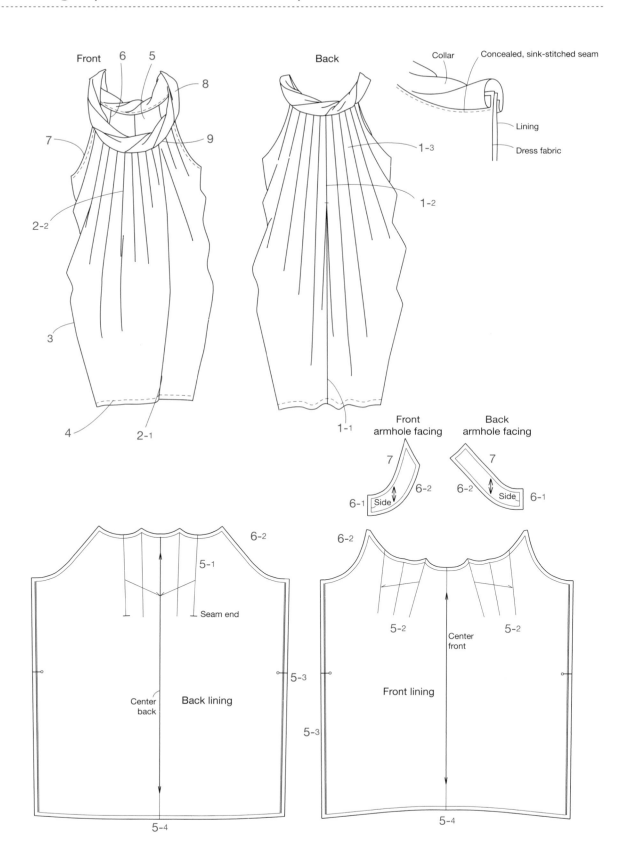

Front

6 5

8

7

9

2-2

3

4 2-1

Back

1-3

1-2

1-1

Collar Concealed, sink-stitched seam

Lining

Dress fabric

Front armhole facing

7

6-1 Side 6-2

Back armhole facing

7

6-2 Side 6-1

6-2

5-1

Seam end

Center back Back lining

5-3

5-3

5-4

6-2

5-2 5-2

Center front

Front lining

5-4

1 Sew the center back and fold the tucks

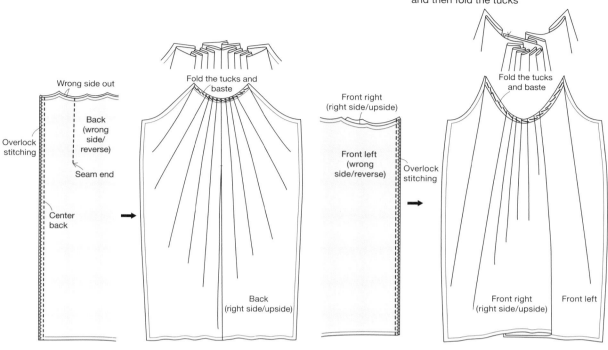

Wrong side out

Overlock stitching

Back (wrong side/reverse)

Seam end

Center back

Fold the tucks and baste

Back (right side/upside)

2 Sew together the left and right sides of the bodice front, and then fold the tucks

Front right (right side/upside)

Front left (wrong side/reverse)

Overlock stitching

Fold the tucks and baste

Front right (right side/upside)

Front left

8 Make the collar

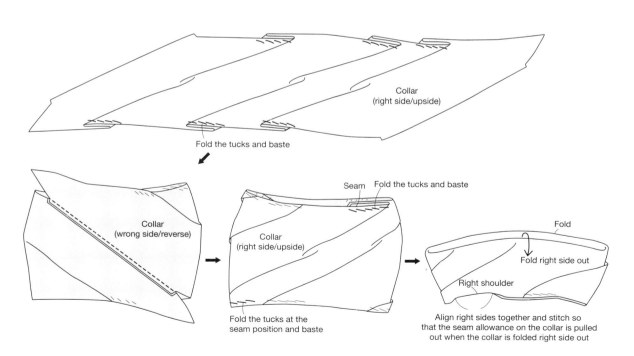

Collar (right side/upside)

Fold the tucks and baste

Collar (wrong side/reverse)

Collar (right side/upside)

Fold the tucks at the seam position and baste

Seam Fold the tucks and baste

Fold

Fold right side out

Right shoulder

Align right sides together and stitch so that the seam allowance on the collar is pulled out when the collar is folded right side out

no. 15 one-piece strapless ruched dress
see page 80 for instructions

no. 15 one-piece strapless ruched dress

◆ **Required pattern pieces (side C)**

1 Bodice (align the top and hem)

◆ **Sewing instructions**

1 Sew and gather the center back
   (see figure 1 on p. 81).
2 Finish the top edge (see figure 2
   on p. 81).
3 Fold up the hem and blind-stitch.

◆ **Widths and lengths used**

Fabric: stretch fabric/Tencel jersey
   (plain knit)
   = W 1 m 50 cm x L 1 m 70 cm

Cutting layout

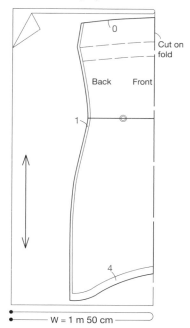

W = 1 m 50 cm

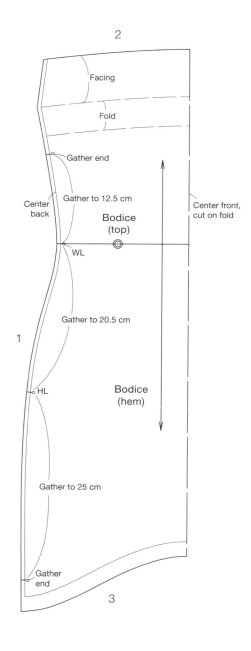

Front

Back

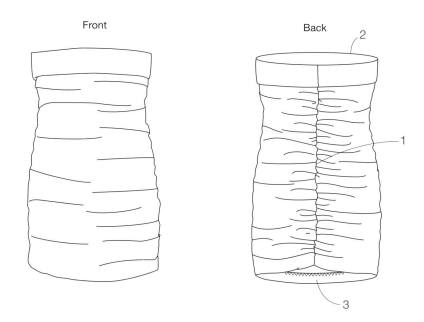

2

1

3

1 Sew and gather the center back

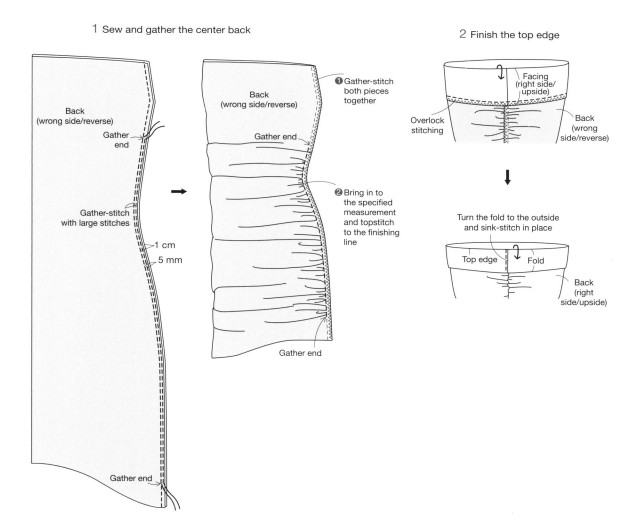

Back
(wrong side/reverse)

Gather
end

Gather-stitch
with large stitches

1 cm

5 mm

Gather end

Back
(wrong side/reverse)

Gather end

❶ Gather-stitch
both pieces
together

❷ Bring in to
the specified
measurement
and topstitch
to the finishing
line

Gather end

2 Finish the top edge

Facing
(right side/
upside)

Overlock
stitching

Back
(wrong
side/reverse)

Turn the fold to the outside
and sink-stitch in place

Top edge

Fold

Back
(right
side/upside)

Bibliography

The Essential Basics of Sewing Beautifully by Keiko Mizuno (BUNKA PUBLISHING BUREAU)

Sewing Lesson Note ABC by Naoko Domeki (BUNKA PUBLISHING BUREAU)

Fashion Dictionary (BUNKA PUBLISHING BUREAU)

Credits

Original Japanese edition

Publisher: Sunao Onuma
Editor: Kayako Hirayama (BUNKA PUBLISHING BUREAU)
Design and layout: Tomoko Nawata, L'Espace
Photography: Yasutomo Ebisu, Josui Yasuda (BUNKA PUBLISHING BUREAU)
Hair and make-up: Hiromi Chinone (Cirque)
Model: Emma B, Katie
Pattern grading: Kazuhiro Ueno
Instructions: Keiko Mizuno (pp. 7–9), Naoko Domeki (pp. 12–81)
Tracing: Tomoko Fukushima
Proofreading: Masako Mukai

English edition

Translated from the Japanese by Andy Walker
Technical consultants: Kevin Almond, Bo Breda, Chika Ito
Design and typesetting: Mark Holt
Commissioning editor: Helen Rochester (Laurence King Publishing)
Editor: Sarah Batten (Laurence King Publishing)